D0627294

Girls Play VOLLEYBALL

Girls
JOIN THE
TEAM

Anne Forest

PowerKiDS press

New York

Published in 2017 by The Rosen Publishing Group, Inc.
29 East 21st Street, New York, NY 10010

First Edition

Editor: Katie Kawa
Book Design: Tanya Dellaccio

Cataloging-in-Publication Data

Names: Forest, Anne.
Title: Girls play volleyball / Anne Forest.
Description: New York : PowerKids Press, 2017. | Series: Girls join the team | Includes index.
Identifiers: ISBN 9781499421118 (pbk.) | ISBN 9781499421132 (library bound) | ISBN 9781499421125 (6 pack)
Subjects: LCSH: Women volleyball players–Juvenile literature. | Women volleyball players–United States–Juvenile literature.
Classification: LCC GV1015.4.W66 F667 2017 | DDC 796.325082–d23

Manufactured in the United States of America

CPSIA Compliance Information: Batch #BS16PK For Further Information contact Rosen Publishing, New York, New York at 1-800-237-9932

CONTENTS

A True Team Sport 4

The Roots of the Game 6

Playing by the Rules 8

Point, Set, Match 10

International Indoor Volleyball 12

Never Too Young! 14

Success on the Sand. 16

Grab Your Gear! 18

From School to the Pros 20

It Takes Teamwork 22

Glossary. 23

Index 24

Websites 24

A TRUE TEAM SPORT

Volleyball started as a sport played in small gyms around the United States, and now it's one of the most popular sports in the world. It was first played more than 100 years ago by American men. Now, it's a sport girls in many countries are playing in larger numbers than ever before.

Volleyball is a great sport for girls to play because it teaches them to work together. To find success, volleyball players must **communicate** with their teammates and trust them to do their part. Read on to learn more about this fun sport and the strong women who play it!

Overtime!

The Fédération Internationale de Volleyball (FIVB), which governs volleyball internationally, is the largest sports **organization** of its kind in the world.

There are two main kinds of volleyball. Indoor volleyball is played on an indoor court. Outdoor volleyball—also called beach volleyball—is played outside on sand.

THE ROOTS OF THE GAME

The history of volleyball starts with the invention of the sport of basketball in Springfield, Massachusetts, in 1891. Some men found basketball to be too tough on their body. With that in mind, William G. Morgan invented an **alternative** to basketball in 1895 in Holyoke, Massachusetts. This sport involved hitting a ball over a net.

Volleyball grew in popularity among men and women in the United States, and it also began to spread around the world. The FIVB was founded in 1947. It held its first world **championship** for men in 1949 and for women in 1952.

Overtime!

Volleyball was called "mintonette" at first. However, its name was changed soon after it was invented. The name "volleyball" came from the fact that the ball is volleyed—or hit back and forth before it touches the ground—during the game.

The governing body for U.S. volleyball—now called USA Volleyball (USAV)—held its first national championship for women in 1949. USAV also puts together the U.S. national teams that compete in international events, including FIVB **competitions**.

PLAYING BY THE RULES

Indoor volleyball is officially played with teams of six—three players in the front row and three players in the back row. Play starts when a member of one team serves the ball over the net to the other team's side of the court.

After a serve, the other team tries to hit the ball back over the net. Play goes back and forth over the net until the ball hits the ground or a fault is **committed**. A team gets a point in volleyball if the ball touches the other team's side of the court inside the **boundary** lines or if the other team commits a fault.

Overtime!

A player keeps serving the ball until her team commits a fault or the other team gets the ball to hit the floor on her side of the court. When that happens, the other team gets a chance to serve. Players then move clockwise one position, so a new player gets a chance to serve next time.

A team is only allowed to hit the ball three times before it has to make it back over the net. Teammates have to work together to keep the ball off the ground.

POINT, SET, MATCH

The first team to score 25 points wins a set in indoor volleyball. However, in order to win a set, a team must win by at least two points. This means a team can't win a set 25–24. The first team to win three sets wins the whole game, or match. If a match has to go to five sets, the winner of the fifth set only needs to score 15 points and win by at least two points.

The rules of indoor volleyball have changed to allow teams to score whether they're the serving team or the team receiving the serve. At one time, only the serving team could earn a point.

Overtime!

One player on each indoor volleyball team wears a jersey, or shirt, that's a different color than those worn by the rest of her team. This player is the libero, and she's a defensive specialist, which means her job is to keep the other team from scoring. She passes the ball and works hard to keep the ball from touching her side of the court.

VOLLEYBALL GLOSSARY

attack

The act of jumping and hitting the ball with an overhand swinging motion. It can also be called a hit.

block

The act of one or more players jumping with their arms reaching above the net to stop the other team from getting the ball over it.

bump

A kind of pass in which a player puts her forearms together to hit the ball to another player.

dig

The act of stopping the ball from hitting the ground by passing it to a teammate.

fault

An error committed by a team that causes the other team to earn a point.

kill

A hit that scores a point because the other team can't return it. It can also be called a spike.

libero

A defensive specialist who plays only in the back row and wears a different color jersey.

rally

The time spent keeping the ball in the air as it moves back and forth over the net—from the serve to the time a point is scored.

serve

The act of hitting the ball over the net to start play.

set

The act of placing the ball near the net to help a teammate get a kill. A set is also a period in a volleyball game that lasts until a team scores 25 points and at least two more points than the other team.

side out

A rally won by the team that received the serve.

These are just some of words you might hear during a volleyball game. Many of these words describe special plays that must be practiced in order to do them well.

INTERNATIONAL INDOOR VOLLEYBALL

Playing volleyball could take you all over the world! Because volleyball is a popular sport in so many countries, international volleyball competitions are major sporting events around the globe. These competitions allow the best volleyball players in the world to face each other. The FIVB hosts events such as world championships and the World Cup for both men's and women's indoor volleyball teams.

Indoor volleyball became an Olympic sport for both men and women at the 1964 Summer Olympics. The U.S. women's indoor volleyball team has had some success in recent Olympics. The Americans won silver **medals** in 2008 and 2012.

Overtime!

As of 2015, the Soviet Union holds the record for the most Olympic gold medals in women's indoor volleyball with four. The Soviet Union was a country that was located in the area that's now Russia and part of Eastern Europe.

The FIVB hosts championships for volleyball players at different ages. It even has a world championship for girls under 18 years old!

Team USA at the FIVB Girls' Under-18 World Championship

Brazil's 2012 Olympic indoor volleyball team with their gold medals

NEVER TOO YOUNG!

If you love to play volleyball, it's never too early to start working toward a place on the U.S. women's national team. Logan Tom became a member of the national team when she was only 16 years old! She then became the youngest player ever to be named to the country's Olympic team. When she was 19 years old, she made the team that played in the 2000 Summer Olympics.

Logan played for the United States in four Olympics. She was part of both U.S. teams that won silver medals. During the 2008 Summer Olympics, she scored 124 points, making her the best women's indoor volleyball scorer at those Olympics.

Overtime!

Logan went to college at Stanford University. She helped that school win a national championship in women's indoor volleyball in 2001.

Logan was a star on the volleyball court and in the classroom as she was growing up. She had the best grades in her high school class!

SUCCESS ON THE SAND

Beach volleyball is also popular in many countries, with the FIVB hosting international competitions for men and women. While this sport started in the United States in the 1920s and 1930s, it didn't become an Olympic sport until the 1996 Summer Olympics.

The United States has more Olympic gold medals in beach volleyball than any other country. Its most successful team—often considered the best in the sport's history—was made up of Misty May-Treanor and Kerri Walsh Jennings. They won three Olympic gold medals in a row at the 2004, 2008, and 2012 Summer Olympics.

Overtime!

Misty and Kerri only lost one set in the 43 Olympic sets they played!

Misty and Kerri played indoor volleyball before finding Olympic success on the sand. One big difference between indoor volleyball and beach volleyball is that beach volleyball teams only have two players.

Misty
May-Treanor

Kerri Walsh
Jennings

FIVB.
FÉDÉRATION INTERNATIONALE
DE VOLLEYBALL
London 2012

London 2012

GRAB YOUR GEAR!

Do you think it would be fun to be a volleyball superstar like Logan, Misty, or Kerri? You don't need much to start a game of volleyball—just a net, a ball, and a place to play. If you go to the beach, some places already have volleyball nets in the sand. All you need to wear to play beach volleyball is your bathing suit. Some beach volleyball players also wear sunglasses.

Indoor volleyball players often wear kneepads. This kind of volleyball sometimes involves diving on a hard floor. This can hurt your knees if you don't use the proper **protection**. Indoor volleyball players also need to wear the right shoes to keep from sliding on the floor.

Overtime!

Some indoor volleyball players wear shorts with padding in them. The padding protects their hips from getting hurt when they dive for the ball.

Because beach volleyball is played on soft sand instead of a hard floor, players don't wear much protection.

FROM SCHOOL TO THE PROS

If volleyball sounds like a sport you'd like to play, ask if your school has an indoor volleyball team you can join. Many communities also have their own girls' indoor volleyball teams, and some of these teams travel around the country to play each other.

Girls who love indoor volleyball can play the sport in college if they work hard enough on the court and in the classroom. Beach volleyball is also becoming a more popular college sport in the United States. There are national college championships for both indoor and beach volleyball.

Overtime!

The United States has its own **professional** volleyball **league**. It's called the Premiere Volleyball League, and it has its own championship for men and women every year.

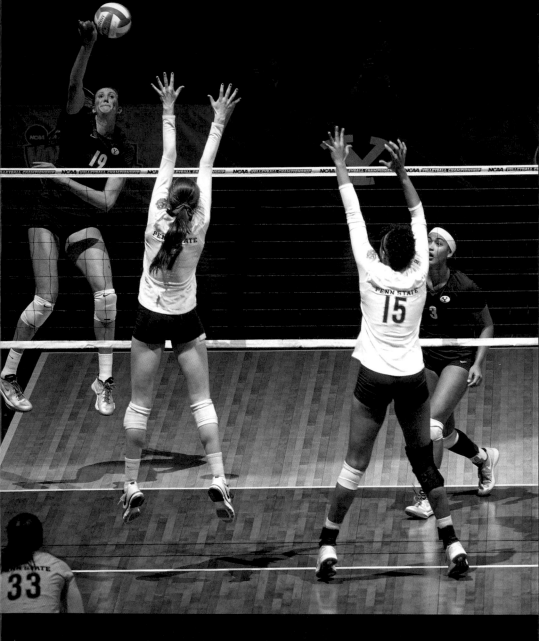

In 2015, more people attended the college women's indoor volleyball championship than ever before!

IT TAKES TEAMWORK

Volleyball isn't a sport you can play on your own. It's a team sport—whether you're playing with a beach volleyball partner, a group of indoor volleyball teammates, or just a bunch of friends in gym class. Because a volleyball player can't hit the ball twice in a row, teamwork is an important part of this sport. Players have to help each other to win a point, a set, and a match.

As the number of girls playing volleyball keeps rising, more girls are learning to work together to do great things. That's what it really means to play like a girl!

GLOSSARY

alternative: Something that can be chosen instead of something else.

boundary: Something that shows where one area ends and another area begins.

championship: A contest to find out who's the best player or team in a sport.

commit: To do something—often something that is wrong.

communicate: To share knowledge or feelings.

competition: An event between two or more people or groups to find a winner.

league: A group of teams that play the same sport and compete against each other.

medal: A flat, small piece of metal with art or words that's used as an honor or reward.

organization: A group formed for a specific purpose.

professional: Having to do with a job someone does for a living.

protection: Something that keeps someone safe.

INDEX

A
attack, 11

B
beach volleyball, 5,
16, 17, 18, 19,
20, 22
block, 11
bump, 11

C
court, 5, 8, 10, 15, 20

D
dig, 11

F
fault, 8, 11
FIVB, 4, 6, 7, 12, 13,
16

I
indoor volleyball, 5,
8, 10, 12, 13,
14, 17, 18, 20,
21, 22

K
kill, 11

L
libero, 10, 11

M
May-Treanor, Misty,
16, 17, 18
mintonette, 6
Morgan, William G.,
6

O
Olympics, 12, 13, 14,
16, 17

P
Premiere Volleyball
League, 20

R
rally, 11

S
serve, 8, 10, 11
set, 10, 11, 16, 22
side out, 11
Soviet Union, 12
Stanford University,
14

T
Tom, Logan, 14, 15,
18

U
United States, 4, 6,
7, 12, 14, 16, 20
USAV, 7

W
Walsh Jennings,
Kerri, 16, 17, 18
World Cup, 12

WEBSITES

Due to the changing nature of Internet links, PowerKids Press has developed
an online list of websites related to the subject of this book. This site is
updated regularly. Please use this link to access the list:
www.powerkidslinks.com/gjt/vball